JOHN PAUL
JONES

Scott Ingram

BLACKBIRCH®
PRESS

THOMSON

GALE

San Diego • Detroit • New York • San Francisco • Cleveland
New Haven, Conn. • Waterville, Maine • London • Munich

THOMSON
GALE

For more information, contact
The Gale Group, Inc.
27500 Drake Rd.
Farmington Hills, MI 48331-3535
Or you can visit our Internet site at http://www.gale.com

LIBRARY OF CONGRESS CATALOGING-IN-PUBLICATION DATA

Ingram, Scott (William Scott)
  John Paul Jones / by W. Scott Ingram.
     v. cm. — (Triangle history of the American Revolution.
Revolutionary War leaders)
  Includes bibliographical references and index.
  Contents: From apprentice to master — From fugitive to lieutenant — Early years of a new navy — Across the Atlantic — The wait and the great battle — A forgotten hero.
  ISBN 1-56711-609-4 (alk. paper)
  1. Jones, John Paul, 1747-1792—Juvenile literature. 2. Admirals—United States—Biography—Juvenile literature. 3. United States. Navy—Biography—Juvenile literature. 4. United States—History—Revolution, 1775-1783—Naval operations—Juvenile literature. [1. Jones, John Paul, 1747-1792. 2. Admirals. 3. United States—History—Revolution, 1775-1783—Naval operations.] I. Title. II. Series.
  E207.J7 I48 2003
  973.3'5'092—dc21   2002003227

Printed in China
10 9 8 7 6 5 4 3 2 1

CONTENTS

PREFACE: THE AMERICAN REVOLUTION

Today, more than two centuries after the final shots were fired, the American Revolution remains an inspiring story not only to Americans, but also to people around the world. For many citizens, the well-known battles that occurred between 1775 and 1781—such as Lexington, Trenton, Yorktown, and others—represent the essence of the Revolution. In truth, however, the formation of the United States involved much more than the battles of the Revolutionary War. The creation of our nation occurred over several decades, beginning in 1763, at the end of the French and Indian War, and continuing until 1790, when the last of the original 13 colonies ratified the Constitution.

More than 200 years later, it may be difficult to fully appreciate the courage and determination of the people who fought for, and founded, our nation. The decision to declare independence was not made easily—and it was not unanimous. Breaking away from England—the ancestral land of most colonists—was a bold and difficult move. In addition to the emotional hardship of revolt, colonists faced the greatest military and economic power in the world at the time.

The first step on the path to the Revolution was essentially a dispute over money. By 1763, England's treasury had been drained in order to pay for the French and Indian War. British lawmakers, as well as England's new ruler, King George III, felt that the colonies should help to pay for the war's expense and for the cost of housing the British troops who remained in the colonies. Thus began a series of oppressive British tax acts and other laws that angered the colonists and eventually provoked full-scale violence.

King George III

    The Stamp Act of 1765 was followed by the Townshend
Acts in 1767. Gradually, colonists were forced to pay
taxes on dozens of everyday goods from playing cards to
paint to tea. At the same time, the colonists had no say in
the passage of these acts. The more colonists complained
that "taxation without representation is tyranny," the
more British lawmakers claimed the right to make laws

for the colonists "in all cases whatsoever." Soldiers and tax collectors were sent to the colonies to enforce the new laws. In addition, the colonists were forbidden to trade with any country but England.

Each act of Parliament pushed the colonies closer to unifying in opposition to English laws. Boycotts of British goods inspired protests and violence against tax collectors. Merchants who continued to trade with the Crown risked attacks by their colonial neighbors. The rising violence soon led to riots against British troops stationed in the colonies and the organized destruction of British goods. Tossing tea into Boston Harbor was just one destructive act. That event, the Boston Tea Party, led England to pass the so-called Intolerable Acts of 1774. The port of Boston was closed, more British troops were sent to the colonies, and many more legal rights for colonists were suspended.

Finally, there was no turning back. Early on an April morning in 1775, at Lexington Green in Massachusetts, the first shots of the American Revolution were fired. Even after the first battle, the idea of a war against England seemed unimaginable to all but a few radicals. Many colonists held out hope that a compromise could be reached. Except for the Battle of Bunker Hill and some minor battles at sea, the war ceased for much of 1775. During this time, delegates to the Continental Congress struggled to reach a consensus about the next step.

During those uncertain months, the Revolution was fought, not on a military battlefield, but on the battlefield of public opinion. Ardent rebels—especially Samuel Adams and Thomas Paine—worked tirelessly to keep the spirit of revolution alive. They stoked the fires of revolt by writing letters and pamphlets, speaking at public gatherings, organizing boycotts, and devising other forms of protest. It was their brave efforts that kept others focused on liberty and freedom until July 4, 1776. On that day, Thomas Jefferson's Declaration of Independence left no doubt about the intentions of the colonies. As John Adams wrote afterward, the "revolution began in hearts and minds not on the battlefield."

As unifying as Jefferson's words were, the United States did not become a nation the moment the Declaration of Independence claimed the right of all people to "life, liberty, and the pursuit of happiness." Before, during, and after the war, Americans who spoke of their "country" still generally meant whatever colony was their home. Some colonies even had their own navies during the war, and a few sent their own representatives to Europe to seek aid for their colony alone while delegates from the Continental Congress were doing the same job for the whole United States. Real national unity did not begin to take hold until the inauguration of George Washington in 1789, and did not fully bloom until the dawn of the 19th century.

The story of the American Revolution has been told for more than two centuries and may well be told for centuries to come. It is a tribute to the men and women who came together during this unique era that, to this day, people the world over find inspiration in the story of the Revolution. In the words of the Declaration of Independence, these great Americans risked "their lives, their fortunes, and their sacred honor" for freedom.

The Minuteman statue stands in Concord, Massachusetts.

Introduction:
"I Shall Be Under the Necessity of Firing"

★ ★ ★ ★ ★

Late in the afternoon of September 23, 1779, a large, three-mast ship slowly sailed past Flamborough Head off the eastern coast of England. The peninsula was a landmark for sailors in the region—its white chalk cliffs, hundreds of feet above the sea, were visible for miles. Deep gullies at the base of the cliffs led to caves that had long been hideouts for pirates. Among the people of the area—in fact, among British citizens everywhere—the pirate they feared most was a slight, sandy-haired Scotsman named John Paul Jones. Jones and his men were not really pirates. They were sailors in the Continental navy of the United States. Jones's daring had made him larger than life to the people of England, although he was relatively unknown back in the young United States.

Long before that September evening, rumors of landing by Jones had spread throughout the English countryside. Despite those rumors, residents near Flamborough Head were not worried about the slow-moving ship a few miles offshore, because it flew a British flag. The royal battleship *Serapis* was sailing the waters.

At that moment, in fact, the *Serapis* was in the waters off Flamborough Head. The British vessel, with 50 cannons, was escorting a fleet of cargo

ships. The
commander of the
Serapis, Captain
Richard Pearson,
was as curious about
the identity of the
three-mast ship now
turning toward him

The rough waters and white cliffs of Flamborough
Head were a landmark for sailors.

as the people on land were. It appeared to Pearson
that the unknown ship was positioning itself for
battle, as it lined up with the *Serapis*.

Pearson was not about to take chances, even if
the approaching ship was flying British colors. He
ordered his gun crews to load the cannons. Two decks
of cannons faced outward. The gunners were ready.

As the two ships came within a pistol shot of
each other, Pearson called out, "What ship is that?"

A voice onboard the unknown ship called back,
"The Princess Royal."

"Where from?" called Pearson.

There was no answer. Pearson repeated the
question. Finally, the British commander called out
a warning: "Answer immediately, or I shall be
under the necessity of firing."

At those words, the captain on the other vessel
gave a signal. The British flag was pulled down,
and the American flag raised in its place. "Fire!"
shouted the slight, sandy-haired commander,
Captain John Paul Jones.

Thus began the greatest naval battle of the
American Revolution.

9

Chapter 1

FROM APPRENTICE TO MASTER

The American Revolution brought many brave men and women into the spotlight of American history. The words and deeds of people such as Paul Revere, Nathan Hale, George Washington, and Molly Pitcher have become American legends. The contribution of John Paul Jones to the nation's independence, however, is sometimes overlooked.

OPPOSITE: Sugarcane, grown in the West Indies by African slaves, played a vital role in England's economy.

Among those who fought, few were braver, more determined, or more successful in battle than Jones. No one uttered more memorable words, and no one did more to bring one branch of the American military into existence. Jones, a Scottish immigrant, became known as the "Father of the United States Navy."

In 1747, Samuel Adams started a society for political debate. The club was called the Whipping-Post Club because its members tongue-lashed the government.

Jones did not begin life with the name by which he is known today. He was born John Paul Jr. in a cottage in southwestern Scotland, on July 6, 1747, the youngest of five children. His father John Paul Sr. was the gardener and groundskeeper at Arbigland, an estate owned by a wealthy nobleman named William Craik. John's mother, Jean, was a housekeeper in the Craik mansion.

The Pauls were poor, but their living conditions were better than those of most working-class people at that time. They lived in a four-room stone cottage on the grounds of the Craik estate. There was plenty of food. The Pauls grew vegetables in the estate gardens and got milk from the estate's livestock. In addition, the Craik estate was near the Solway Firth, a huge saltwater inlet between Scotland and England that provided salmon and other fish.

Little is known of John Paul's early life except that he spent most of his free time fishing on the shores of the Solway Firth or exploring the docks in the nearby port town of Dumfries. There he saw

12

the fleets of large sailing ships that brought tobacco and cotton from the American colonies and returned with cloth, tools, tea, and other products for colonists to buy. His childhood playmates recalled that young John Paul liked to arrange rowboat battles with his friends. During these battles, the small, freckled boy assumed the role of commander and shouted orders to the others.

In 1761, at age 13, John packed a wooden chest and said good-bye to his parents. He boarded a fishing boat that took him to the English port of Whitehaven. There he signed the papers of apprenticeship that required him to serve in the fleet of a local merchant, John Younger, for seven years. John Paul would receive little pay for his work, but he would learn the basics of seamanship and navigation. Once the papers were signed, John boarded the *Friendship* and set sail across the Atlantic Ocean as the cabin boy for Captain Robert Benson.

Growing Up at Sea and on Land

The *Friendship*, like many British merchant ships of the time, followed the same route on every journey. The first stop was Barbados, an island in the British West Indies. The most important crop grown in Barbados, and in other British colonies in the Caribbean region, was sugarcane. The crop was worked by African slaves on plantations much like the tobacco plantations of the American southern colonies. The cane was harvested and

13

processed to make sugar, molasses, and rum, three widely used products in the American colonies.

From Barbados, the *Friendship* sailed north to the Chesapeake Bay and up the Rappahannock River to the river port of Fredericksburg, Virginia. There the cane and cane products from Barbados were unloaded and sold. A new cargo of tobacco, cotton, and plank lumber was loaded onboard for the return trip to Whitehaven.

The stops in Fredericksburg did a great deal to relieve the teenage cabin boy's homesickness. John's older brother, William, had opened a tailor shop in the busy city and was happily settled there. The young sailor's apprentice was glad to be able to stay with his brother and avoid the rough sailor's life that he had seen on shore in Barbados.

The pattern of voyages from England to the West Indies to Virginia continued for the first three years of John's apprenticeship. Because sailing vessels had to wait until favorable winds allowed them to leave Virginia, many months sometimes passed before the ship could sail back to Whitehaven. As a result, John spent the entire summer of 1762 with William while he waited for favorable sailing conditions. During that time, and on other visits to Fredericksburg, he learned proper manners and speech from his brother's upper-class customers, who were the wealthiest and best-educated men of the colonies. He lost his heavy Scottish accent and learned to speak grammatically.

★
In 1762, Abigail and John Adams became engaged to marry.
★

He also used his time ashore to improve his reading and writing abilities.

John received a different kind of education during the six-week voyages across the Atlantic Ocean. He learned to navigate by reading the position of the stars. He also learned how to pull in or let out the many sails on the *Friendship* to gain speed or avoid losing control in high winds— a skill known as rigging. Perhaps most important, John learned that the master of the ship might be required to use the strongest discipline to maintain order onboard. He witnessed several floggings of seamen who broke ship rules.

By the time he was 17, John had acquired an education—both on shore and at sea—that was better than that of most young men of his day. His apprenticeship came to an end in 1764. Upon their return to Whitehaven, Benson and the crew discovered that their employer, John Younger, had gone out of business. The *Friendship* was sold to pay the merchant's debts. Younger was forced to lay off Benson and the rest of the seamen.

"Abominable Trade"

Paul found himself jobless in Whitehaven. The British economy was in a depression, and there were more able-bodied seamen in the port than there were jobs. Only one type of cargo ship was always in need of crew. These were the ships that carried human cargo—slave ships, known as "slavers."

A diagram from the eighteenth century
shows how closely slaves were kept
together during the dreadful voyage
from Africa to America.

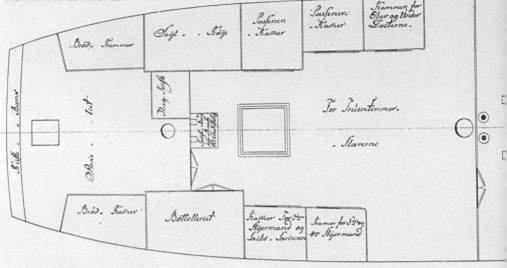

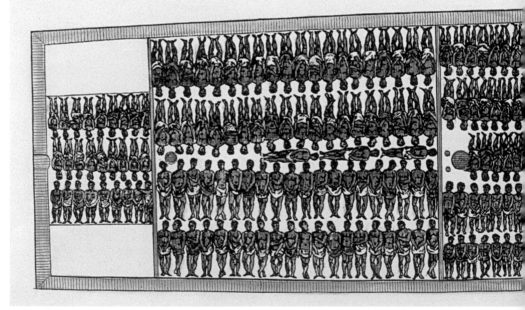

John Paul Jones

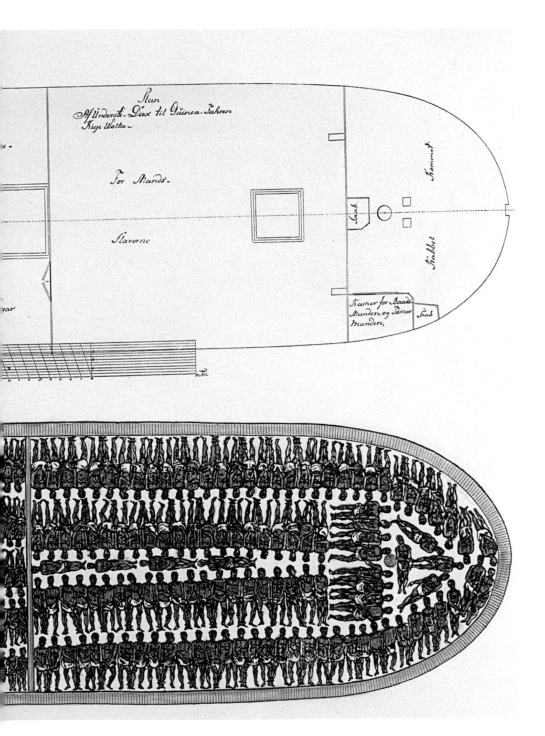

17

In 1764, Paul signed on as a third mate on the *King George*, a slaver based in Whitehaven. The ship sailed from England to the west coast of Africa. There, more than 75 slaves were chained below decks on the 50-foot long vessel, where they would remain for weeks during the long ocean crossing. The *King George* then sailed to Kingston, Jamaica, another British possession in the Caribbean, which was a center of slave trade in the British West Indies. After the crew of the *King George* unloaded the slaves that had survived the trip, the ship took on a cargo of sugar and returned to Whitehaven.

Although he hated the work on the slave ship, it was the only employment that Paul could find for several years. In that time, he worked his way up to chief mate. Finally, after three years, he could no longer endure being part of what he called the "abominable trade." After his arrival in Kingston from Africa in 1768, Paul asked to be relieved of his duties. The *King George* sailed from Kingston and left him behind. He hoped to catch a ride on a regular cargo ship back to Whitehaven and look for other work there.

As luck would have it, the *John*, a British ship, arrived in Kingston in July 1768 with a cargo of salted beef from Ireland. Paul was delighted to learn that the captain of the ship, Samuel McAdam, was an old acquaintance from Scotland. The captain offered the young mate a free trip back to Whitehaven, and he happily accepted.

18

An unusual turn of events occurred on the return voyage when both McAdam and his chief mate died from illness. The only person onboard who knew anything about navigation and sail rigging was Paul. He took command and guided the ship and its crew safely to England.

The owners of the *John* considered themselves fortunate to have their ship return to port safely, and they immediately saw that Paul had a talent for command. The *John*'s owners appointed Paul the master of the vessel and added the title of "supercargo." This gave Paul the right to buy and sell cargo at any time during the voyage. So, at age 21, Paul was the captain—a "master" in the language of the merchant trade—of a cargo vessel in the West Indies trade route.

Chapter 2

FROM FUGITIVE TO LIEUTENANT

Although Paul's early career took him to the American colonies, there is no record of his attitude toward the growing unrest among many of the colonists at the time. His initial years as an apprentice came at the end of the Seven Years' War between England and France—a war that Great Britain won, but at great cost. At the end of that war, the British were deeply in debt. Because the British people were already heavily taxed, the British Parliament felt that the colonists should pay for the costs of the war, which was largely fought in North America.

OPPOSITE: The Liberty Tree in Boston was a place for colonists who opposed British taxes to gather and protest.

Growing Anger in the Colonies

In 1764, as Paul began his work on a slaver, Parliament passed the controversial Sugar Act. This act forced colonists to pay a duty—a form of tax— on any sugar that came into the colonies from places other than the British West Indies. This act was the first of several laws over the next decade that forced colonists to buy only British goods.

The Sugar Act was followed by the Stamp Act, which caused even greater outrage among colonists. This law taxed all paper goods used by colonists. Anyone who needed a document, such as a marriage license, a bill of sale, or a diploma, had to pay an extra tax for it. All newspapers, magazines, calendars, postage stamps, and even playing cards had to have the king's seal, or stamp, on them, as a sign that the tax had been paid. Those who refused to pay were jailed and tried without a jury.

Colonists from New Hampshire to Georgia rebelled against the Stamp Act. But nowhere was the anger greater than in the Massachusetts port city of Boston. There, under the leadership of Samuel Adams, colonists organized as the Sons of Liberty. These young men attacked and beat British tax collectors. They also destroyed the offices of any merchants who imported taxable British goods.

This rebellion by the colonists was unexpected and frightening to both British lawmakers and royalty. By 1767, more than two million people lived in the colonies. That was almost one-quarter of the population of England. The fact that the colonists had begun to call themselves Americans and assert their right to have a voice in their government caught the British by surprise.

In response to colonial protests, the British repealed the Stamp Act. England still wanted money from the colonies, however, and in 1767, Parliament passed the Townshend Acts. These laws taxed almost all goods that were imported by the colonies, including lead, glass, paper, paint, and tea. The colonists were not only forced to buy only British goods, they also had to pay an extra tax simply to bring them into the colonies.

By 1769, colonial merchants in Boston, New York, Philadelphia, and Charleston had agreed to a boycott of all British goods. This created hardship in the colonies, but by 1770, British exports to the colonies had been reduced almost by half. The plan to raise money had actually hurt the British economy.

The British response to the actions of the colonists only worsened relations between the two sides. Parliament sent British troops to the colonies, and stationed most of them in Boston. The troops were supposed to enforce order and aid tax collectors. This move played into the hands of Samuel Adams. As soon as troops arrived, Adams began to organize protests against the British military presence. British troops, called lobster-backs because of their red uniform coats, were insulted and harassed everywhere they went.

23

The Boston Massacre in 1770 enraged American colonists.

Finally, on the night of March 5, 1770, a crowd of colonists began to throw snowballs and threaten a group of soldiers. Cornered by an angry mob of colonists, the soldiers feared for their lives. Musket fire broke out, and when the smoke cleared, five colonists were dead.

Samuel Adams spread the word throughout the colonies about what he called the Boston Massacre. He claimed that cruel British soldiers had fired on innocent colonists. The truth was much more complicated, but Adams's description was the one accepted in the colonies, and it led to even stronger anti-British feeling among Americans.

British lawmakers, aware that the boycott and the violence were hurting the nation, repealed the Townshend Acts. As a sign of their right to impose taxes, however, Parliament kept the tax on tea. For most colonists, this one relatively small tax was acceptable. Merchants lifted their boycotts, and trade between England and the colonies resumed.

For people such as Samuel Adams, however, whose ultimate goal was colonial independence from England, the repeal of the Townshend Acts did little. Adams continued to correspond with other anti-British colonists, such as Thomas Jefferson and Patrick Henry of Virginia.

Patrick Henry was an outspoken advocate of liberty.

By 1773, Adams and anti-British leaders in other colonies had formed groups called Committees of Correspondence to communicate information about anti-British activities in various regions.

A Merchant in the West Indies

For his part, Paul managed to avoid being caught between the American colonists and the British. His voyages in command of the *John* took the ship from Whitehaven to the British West Indies and back. Beginning in 1768, Paul made one or two voyages a year between the two points. The *John* was a small ship with a crew of just seven men. Paul was the sole person in charge of navigation and rigging. He was also in charge of the discipline on board, which mainly meant keeping his crew from eating or drinking any of the ship's cargo.

Among the rough, rugged sailors, Paul stood out in several ways. He had grown to his full height of five feet five inches tall. He dressed like a gentleman, in a style much like those of the men he had seen in his brother's tailor shop. On voyages, he wore a uniform and carried a sword on his belt, more like a naval officer than a merchant master.

During his free time onboard or ashore, Paul read classic literature such as the works of William Shakespeare. He also enjoyed writing poetry. Yet despite his size, dress, and hobbies, Paul was known mainly for his fierce temper. It was not unusual for a slow-moving crewman to receive a kick in the pants from the skipper. This aspect of his personality caused Paul trouble for much of his career at sea.

The first time his temper caused notice was in 1770, on a voyage to Tobago in the West Indies. During this voyage, the ship's carpenter, a man named Mungo Maxwell, was continually disrespectful to Paul. Finally, the captain had Maxwell tied to the mainmast, then whipped him with a cat-o'-nine-tails, which caused deep cuts in Maxwell's back.

When the ship docked in Tobago, Maxwell complained to the naval authorities in the port about Paul's action. Paul told the harbormaster that Maxwell was disobedient and incompetent. The harbormaster threw out the complaint, and Maxwell shipped home on another cargo vessel.

On the return voyage, Maxwell died from unknown causes. His father, a local politician in England, blamed his son's death on "wounds and bruizes . . . by John Paul" and filed a murder charge against the captain. When Paul arrived in Whitehaven, he was immediately charged with murder and thrown in jail.

★
In the fall of 1770, John Adams successfully defended the British soldiers accused of murder in the Boston Massacre.
★

Paul soon arranged bail. At the trial, the captain of the ship on which Maxwell died testified that the carpenter had been in fine health when the ship left Tobago. Paul was acquitted, but the story that he had whipped a sailor to death followed him for the rest of his life.

27

Success and Misfortune

Paul continued to sail between England and the West Indies for several years after the Maxwell incident, but eventually the merchant owners of the *John* had to sell the ship because the American boycott had affected their profits. In 1772, a London-based merchant company gave Paul the command of a large, square-sailed ship, the *Betsy*. The young Scotsman was so skillful at buying and selling cargo that he became a co-owner of the *Betsy* within a year. By age 26, he was on his way to a successful career and great wealth.

Paul's growing success, however, was cut short by an incident that he described in a letter as "the greatest misfortune of my life." In October

London was one of the wealthiest cities in the world during the 1700s.

1773, the *Betsy* docked in Tobago. After he sold the cargo he brought from England, Paul wanted to use the money to buy cargo for the return voyage, in hopes of increasing his profits with the sale of raw materials in England. His crew wanted him to pay them their wages then because they had no intention of making a return trip to England. Most were natives of Tobago and wanted to take the money home to their families.

Paul refused to pay and promised the men a bonus in addition to their salary for making the voyage to England. One man, whom Paul later identified only as the ringleader, organized the crew to demand their wages. They confronted Paul on the deck of the *Betsy*. Paul offered the men some fine cloth to take ashore and give to their wives and girlfriends, but they refused to accept it. The ringleader became so enraged at the offer that he pushed Paul toward a hatchway. Paul drew his sword to warn the man, whom he called "thrice my size," to stop, but this only made the man angrier. He charged, and Paul was forced to run him through with his sword. The man died instantly.

In that moment, the life of John Paul changed forever. No longer was he on the path to wealth as a merchant. Had he killed an English seaman, it is likely that he would have been acquitted as he was in the Maxwell trial. The ringleader, however, was a native of the very island where the *Betsy* was docked. Word of his death spread through the town and crowds began to gather on the dock. The islanders vastly outnumbered the British in Tobago.

The governor urged Paul to leave as quickly as possible because he could not help him. Paul grabbed as much money as he could carry and fled by horseback to a port on the opposite side of Tobago.

No records exist of John Paul's whereabouts between October 1773 and July 1774. Then, a man who called himself John Paul Jones appeared in Fredericksburg, Virginia, to settle the estate of William Paul, a tailor who had died that year. At some point between leaving the *Betsy* and appearing in Fredericksburg, John Paul became John Paul Jones.

The Road to Revolution

During the early 1770s, while Paul sailed between England and the West Indies, the American colonies continued to resist their British rulers. The Virginia that John Paul Jones entered in 1774 was much different from the colony that he had left a decade before. Virginians, even wealthy men such as Thomas Jefferson and Patrick Henry, were urging their fellow Americans to break free from the British.

Farther north in Boston, one event pushed the colonies even closer to revolution. In December 1773, a few months after John Paul disappeared, Bostonians revolted against the Crown in one of the most famous incidents in American history—the Boston Tea Party. This protest occurred as a result of British tax policies toward the colonies and their determination to force colonists to buy English goods.

The Boston Tea Party came about because the British East India Company had an oversupply of tea to sell, but did not have the money to pay the import taxes in England. Parliament wanted to help the company and make money for its treasury as well. The lawmakers decided to let the company sell the tea to the American colonists without paying any duty. The money would be made up by the tea taxes the colonists paid. The colonists would benefit, according to British reasoning, because the cost of the tea would be lower than the tea they smuggled in illegally.

Most colonists did not see it that way at all. To have tea forced on them was one more example of how they lacked a voice in their own affairs. In Boston, where the spirit of independence seemed strongest, Samuel Adams organized a protest. On December 16, 1773, a group of men disguised as Mohawk Indians climbed aboard tea ships in Boston Harbor and dumped 342 chests of tea overboard.

The Boston Tea Party drew a swift response from England. In a series of laws the Parliament called the Coercive Acts—and that the colonists called the "Intolerable Acts"—the port of Boston was closed. The acts no longer allowed towns to hold meetings to settle local matters. They also declared that colonial officials who were accused of crimes must be tried in England. Finally, the acts

Defiant colonists tossed British tea into Boston Harbor on December 16, 1773.

gave British troops the right to live free of charge in the homes of colonists.

The Intolerable Acts did more to unite the colonies than any other action of the British government. In September 1774, 12 of the 13 colonies—only Georgia abstained—sent delegates to the Continental Congress to prepare the colonists' response to British policies. Among the delegates were men such as Adams, Henry, and Jefferson who wanted to break completely away from England. Others, such as Benjamin Franklin, hoped to reach a compromise that would keep ties to England but still allow the colonies some form of self-government.

★

In 1774, General Charles Cornwallis was the vice treasurer of Ireland and was stationed in the Irish city of Cork.

★

In the end, Congress agreed to a colony-wide boycott of British goods. Committees were established to make sure all colonies followed the boycott. The delegates, led by Samuel Adams's cousin, John Adams, also issued a Declaration of Rights and Grievances. This document said that the colonies had a right to pass their own tax laws and denied that the British Parliament had any right to govern them.

As the year 1775 arrived, many colonists were hopeful that an understanding could be reached with the British. Many others, however, were determined to break free of British rule. No colony had been controlled more forcefully by the British than Massachusetts. Many of the colonists there believed that war with England was only a matter

34

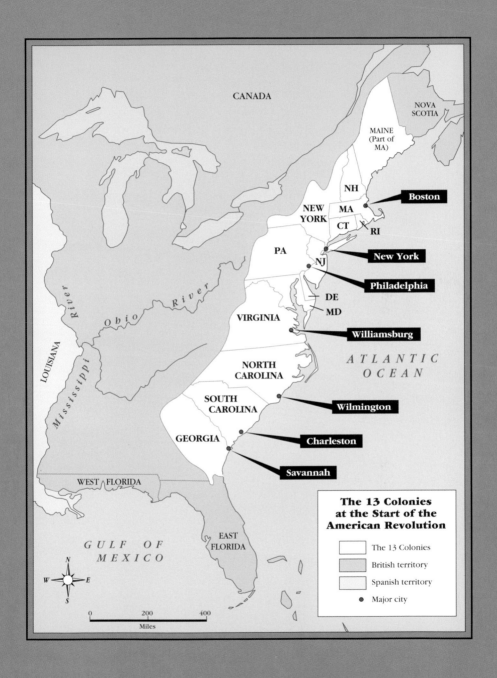

CANADA

NOVA
SCOTIA

MAINE
(Part of
MA)

NH

NEW
YORK

MA

CT

RI

Boston

PA

NJ

New York

Philadelphia

DE

MD

VIRGINIA

Williamsburg

ATLANTIC
OCEAN

NORTH
CAROLINA

SOUTH
CAROLINA

Wilmington

GEORGIA

Charleston

Savannah

LOUISIANA

Ohio River

Mississippi River

WEST FLORIDA

GULF OF
MEXICO

EAST
FLORIDA

N
W   E
S

0   200   400

Miles

**The 13 Colonies
at the Start of the
American Revolution**

The 13 Colonies

British territory

Spanish territory

● Major city

of time, and they began to prepare for battle. Weapons and other military supplies were gathered in Concord, about 20 miles west of Boston. All around the area, local men began military drills to prepare them to respond to a British attack at a moment's notice. These civilians became known as "minutemen."

Massachusetts was not the only colony that was moving toward revolution. The largest and wealthiest colony, Virginia, also took steps toward war and independence. In March 1775, Patrick Henry, who was called the "Samuel Adams of Virginia," gave a rousing speech to his fellow Virginians in favor of independence from England. He concluded the speech with the words, "I know not what path others may take, but as for me, give me liberty or give me death!"

Less than a month later, the first shots of the American Revolution were fired on Lexington Green, between Boston and Concord. Early on the morning of April 19, British troops had left Boston to destroy the colonists' military supplies and to capture Samuel Adams, who was staying in the area. The Battle of Lexington and Concord was the result of this action, and news of the event spread rapidly through the colonies.

A Continental Naval Officer

Throughout this time of turmoil, John Paul Jones was concerned more with his own personal matters than with those of the colonists. From his home in

The first shots of the
American Revolution were
fired on Lexington Green
early on April 19,1775.

Fredericksburg, he traveled north to Philadelphia and south to Charleston, South Carolina, to seek command of a merchant ship. Merchants, however, had little work in those times, and Jones was forced to live on the money he had been able to take from Tobago.

In 1775, Jones met a local woman named Dorothea Dandridge, the daughter of wealthy plantation owner. Although the two discussed marriage, Dandridge's parents would not accept a Scottish immigrant as a son-in-law. They forbid their daughter to continue seeing Jones. A short time later, Dandridge married Patrick Henry, a widower more than 20 years older than she.

Discouraged, heartbroken, and nearly bankrupt, Jones decided to return to the place he knew best—

Esek Hopkins was appointed the commodore—the commander—of the Continental navy.

the sea. By the summer of 1775, the colonies had formed the Continental army under the command of George Washington and the Continental navy under the command of Esek Hopkins. Jones learned that officers were needed for the new navy, so he headed to Philadelphia, the center of resistance in the colonies.

In Philadelphia, Jones appeared before the Marine Committee, a group of colonists who, with Hopkins, were interviewing and appointing officers to the navy. Jones presented himself as one who loved liberty and was determined to fight for freedom. His words, appearance, and knowledge persuaded the committee to offer him a command. In December 1775, John Paul Jones, Esq., was commissioned as the first lieutenant in the Continental navy. Jones was given temporary command of the ship *Alfred*, and he began to prepare it for battle as soon he received the appointment.

SEAMAN OF THE REVOLUTION.

Chapter 3

EARLY YEARS OF
A NEW NAVY

Jones soon discovered that he faced a formidable challenge. Like almost every other aspect of the new nation that became the United States, the Continental navy was slow to take shape. At the outbreak of the Revolution, the United States did not have any warships. Instead, merchant ships of all sizes and levels of seaworthiness were converted into fighting vessels. Sailors came from a variety of backgrounds that varied from fishing boats to slavers. There was no naval war tradition among seaman in the colonies that could equal that of the powerful British navy.

OPPOSITE: Sailors in the Continental navy came from a variety of backgrounds and had little training in naval warfare.

In fact, the first colonial naval force was a fleet of privately owned vessels that were sent out to harass British merchant ships in the fall of 1775. While Jones was in Philadelphia to apply for a commission before the Marine Committee, individual colonies recruited vessels to sail as so-called privateers. Because the British navy was the most powerful in the world, privateers avoided battles with the British warships. Their targets were lightly armed British merchant ships whose heavy loads slowed them down enough that they could be chased and captured. Privateers were essentially pirate ships that operated with a government's permission.

Privateers usually set out on voyages with extra crew onboard. When a privateer captured a British merchant ship—called a prize—the extra crew boarded the prize. In some cases, some of the captured crew might be brought aboard a privateer to perform basic seaman's duties. The prize crew usually replaced the captain, the first mate, and other key positions aboard the captured ship. These men directed the captured ship's crew to sail the ship to port. The privateer, meanwhile, sailed on in search of additional prizes. Eventually, a privateer returned to port when it no longer had enough crew members to spare to man prizes.

Back in port, a prize master kept records of captured ships and goods that were sent back by individual privateers. The prize master arranged for the sale of the prize goods and divided the profits

Privateers boarded ships that they captured and sailed the prize ships back to a friendly port.

according to a prearranged formula. The captured ship itself might be sold to the Continental navy to be outfitted with guns to make it a fighting vessel.

In the 1700s, the capture of merchant vessels in the open seas was a common practice by both privateers and naval vessels in countries as large as Great Britain or as small as the Arab empires of North Africa's Barbary Coast. Many British admirals built enormous fortunes from prize money. Lower-ranking officers often earned two or three times their basic wages on a successful voyage. Even regular crewmen might receive large sums of money. The British navy, which was often

43

A Sailing Warship

★ ★ ★ ★ ★

During the American Revolution, most ships—British, American, or French—carried similar types of weapons for battles at sea. The largest weapons on a sailing ship were the cannons. The size of a cannon was designated by the weight of the cannonball it fired—four-pound, six-pound, and nine-pound were the most common-sized cannons. The largest gun in the American navy was an 18-pounder. Cannonballs were usually fired into the hull of an enemy ship to shatter the wooden sides. The best shots were those that struck the hull below the waterline, because they could quickly sink a ship.

Cannons also fired other types of shot besides round cannonballs. Chainshot was two cannonballs linked by a short chain. Grapeshot was a canister filled with lead shot. Both chainshot and grapeshot were used to rip holes in sail rigging or to kill enemy sailors on deck.

Every man-of-war also carried smaller guns mounted on swivels that could be carried to the top of the masts or moved around on deck to fire at the enemy. Every fighting ship carried a group of men, called marines, whose job was to fight from the tops of the masts or to attack enemy ships by boarding them when the ships were close enough. Marines were equipped with muskets, pistols, and swords. In many cases, they threw grenades—glass bottles filled with gun-powder and metal scraps—down onto the decks of enemy ships to kill the enemy, start fires, or blow up gunpowder supplies.

Marines did most of the hand-to-hand fighting when ships drew next to each other in a battle or when a ship was boarded and captured. American marines often wore thick strips of leather on the back of their necks to protect them from swords during battle. For that reason, marines have been called leathernecks up to modern times.

Cannons extended from gunports to fire at enemy ships.

short of recruits, allowed the officers and crews of warships to keep all of the prize money they earned on a voyage as an incentive to remain in the service.

In contrast to this practice, the Marine Committee, who needed money for its new force, declared that American naval ships could only keep half of the prize money generated. The other half went to the operation of the force or to the Continental treasury.

Because the privateers offered a greater share of prize money and lacked the stern discipline of the navy, they were much more attractive than the Continental navy to most seamen. Recruiting crews for the navy, therefore, proved extremely difficult. Yet, even faced with such difficulties, Jones was determined to assemble and train a disciplined crew for the *Alfred*.

Winter had set in by the time the new lieutenant stepped onto the decks of the *Alfred*. The Delaware River was filled with huge chunks of ice, so the *Alfred* remained anchored in Philadelphia's harbor. Jones's crew was not a trained fighting force, so the young lieutenant used the winter months to "exercise the guns"—he trained his men to load and fire the cannons.

The *Alfred* had a crew of 220 men, including marines, and carried 30 cannons—20 nine-pounders and 10 six-pounders. Coordinating the firing of the guns took a great deal of practice because there were many steps involved, and a crew had to work smoothly as a team. Despite the freezing temperatures, Jones drilled his crew day after day during his first weeks in charge, and had them perform each step in the firing process to the beat of a drum.

The *Alfred*'s cannons sat on low wooden-wheeled carriages. Gun crews used thick ropes around the wheels to move the guns in and out of the gun ports—wooden openings that allowed the muzzles to extend out from the sides of the ship.

Before the firing exercises began, crews placed all of the gun equipment within easy reach. Cannonballs and canvas bags of gunpowder were piled side by side. The powder bags were resupplied by a powder monkey, the youngest gun crew member, who got them from the area called the magazine, below the decks. Other pieces of equipment included a rammer, a sponge, a tub of water, a powder horn, and matches.

At Jones's order "Cast loose your guns," any ropes that secured the cannon in place were removed and coiled. Next came the command "Level your guns," which required gunners to make certain the barrel was parallel to the deck. Next, the corklike stoppers in the muzzles were removed. With the command "Load with cartridge," a bag of powder was rammed down the cannon barrel. "Shot your gun," was the signal to load the cannonball or shot in the cannon.

Next, gun crews were ordered to "run your guns," which meant to pull them to the gun port until the muzzles extended past the hull. Gunners then poured gunpowder from the powder horn into a hole drilled into the top of the cannon above the point where the powder bag sat. A match was lit and the gun aimed. On a ship rolling in ocean waves, aiming was not an easy task. Many shots ended up going into the water or flying over an enemy vessel. Finally, at the command "Fire," the match was touched to the powder hole, which fired the cannon. The recoil of the cannon, sometimes 10 feet or more, kicked it back far enough from the gun port to allow it be reloaded. Before that took place, however, a sponge attached to the end of a pole was dipped into the tub of water and rammed down the muzzle to put out any scraps of the powder bag still burning.

★

In January 1776, *Common Sense,* a pamphlet in support of declaring independence, was written by Thomas Paine.

★

Once the firing exercise was finished, the cannons were pulled back from the ports and lashed in place. One of the most dangerous mishaps that occurred on ships in those days was for a cannon to break free of its lashing. "Loose cannon on deck" was a warning that filled sailors with terror.

After months of drills, Jones had made his untrained seamen into top-notch gun crews. Then, in midwinter 1776, the captain of the *Alfred,* Dudley Saltonstall, arrived to take command. Saltonstall took an immediate dislike to Jones. As a descendent of wealthy New England families, he looked down on Jones as a low-class immigrant.

48

First Action

In the early spring of 1776, the Delaware River thawed enough to allow the *Alfred* and several other Continental ships to sail south into the Chesapeake Bay. The fleet had received orders to sail to British outposts in the Bahamas. There, they were to capture weapons and other supplies for George Washington's newly formed army.

The fleet set sail in March, several months before the Declaration of Independence officially made the colonists' revolt a war for liberty. The ships of the Continental navy did not even have the flag of the United States to identify their country of origin. Instead, they flew the British Union Jack, the flag of the country whose outposts they were under orders to attack.

The American fleet approached the island settlement of Nassau in late March. Because the waters were shallow, the larger ships could not get within cannon range. Instead, a landing party of marines went ashore and took control of the settlement without a struggle. Although the Americans captured more than 100 cannons and thousands of cannonballs, the mission was unsuccessful in one respect. The British commander of the fort had suspected that the approaching fleet was not friendly. He quickly loaded most of the gunpowder that was stored at the settlement into two smaller sailing vessels that had escaped unseen before the Americans landed.

By April 1776, the American fleet was sailing toward Rhode Island from Nassau with the captured military supplies. At that time, the British navy had a large fleet of warships in Narragansett Bay. These ships were intended to prevent American privateers from leaving the large Rhode Island ports of Newport and Bristol. On April 6, the American fleet passed Block Island, located south of Narragansett Bay on the northern end of Long Island Sound. There, the fleet encountered the British vessel *Glasgow*, a ship of 20 guns heading south.

The commander of the *Glasgow* immediately sensed trouble and turned his ship so that his port broadside faced the oncoming Americans. That allowed the British ship to fire all 10 guns on one side while the Americans could only fire swivel guns from their bows. The lack of battle skills among the American commanders made it difficult for them to maneuver several boats into fighting positions.

The *Glasgow* waited until the lead American ship, the *Cabot*, was within range. Then the British ship let loose two broadsides of nine-pounders, which wounded the *Cabot*'s captain, killed several crewmen, and damaged the steering rudder. All the *Cabot* could do was sail helplessly past the British ship.

The *Alfred* was the next ship in the group, and Saltonstall was able to maneuver it so that its broadside faced the *Glasgow*. With Jones commanding the guns, the well-trained crew sprang into action. The British and American ships began to trade broadsides at close range. The other American ships could not get close enough to join the battle for fear of either hitting the *Alfred* or being struck by a wild shot.

Cannons roared, and smoke drifted

Benjamin Franklin, John Adams, Thomas Jefferson, and other delegates formed the committee that drafted the Declaration of Independence.

across the water in the chilly night air. In a fight that lasted nearly an hour, both ships were damaged but continued to fire. Then a broadside from the *Glasgow* struck the *Alfred* below the waterline, punching a hole in the hull and damaging the rudder. The American ship was temporarily disabled, and the crew of the *Glasgow*, aware that they were outnumbered, turned back for Narragansett Bay. The other Americans chased the British ship, but their holds were so heavily loaded with captured cannons that they could not catch it.

51

This skirmish was the first naval encounter of
the Revolution. It showed Jones and other
commanders how much work the Continental
navy needed to do to become a true fighting force.
The ships involved in the fight had barely been
able to avoid one another as they maneuvered to
gain advantage over the enemy ship. Even so,
Jones's performance made an impression on other
commanders. On May 10, 1776, Commodore Esek
Hopkins promoted Jones to captain and gave him
command of the ship *Providence*.

First Independent Missions

The *Providence* was a different type of ship than
the *Alfred*. Jones's first ship was a three-mast brig,
nearly 180 feet long, that carried 30 cannons and a
crew of 220 men. The *Providence* was a single-mast
sloop, 70 feet long, with a crew of 73 that included
extra men for prize crews. It carried 12 four-pound
cannons. Jones actually preferred smaller ships,
such as sloops, because they were easier to maneuver
and could sail in shallower water.

Jones spent several weeks repairing the ship
in its home port of Providence, then sailed to
Philadelphia to take on ammunition and other
supplies. He arrived in the city on August 1,
1776, less than a month after the signing of the
Declaration of Independence. The American War
of Independence was now official. Jones proudly
stood before the Maritime Committee of the
Continental Congress as his orders were read:

In the Navy

In 1776, the Continental Congress published the Naval Pay List. The document listed not only the pay for navy officers and enlisted men, it also offered a "mess list," the daily food allowance for each man.

A captain's salary was $32 per month. Lieutenants earned $20, and junior petty officers earned up to $15 per month. Experienced or "able" seamen earned $9 a month. "Landsmen," or recruits, earned $6.66.

For food, each man received a daily ration of one pound of bread, a pound of beef or pork, a pound of potatoes, and a half-pint of rum. Butter and cheese were offered three times a week and pudding was on the menu twice a week.

"We have ordered the provisions and stores you requested to be put on board the sloop Providence which you command under authority of the United States of America.... The...sloop being ready for sea, you are to proceed immediately on a cruise against our enemies."

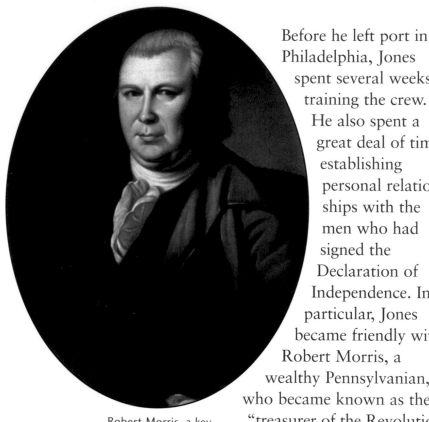

Robert Morris, a key supporter of Jones, was a wealthy delegate to the Continental Congress.

Before he left port in Philadelphia, Jones spent several weeks training the crew. He also spent a great deal of time establishing personal relationships with the men who had signed the Declaration of Independence. In particular, Jones became friendly with Robert Morris, a wealthy Pennsylvanian, who became known as the "treasurer of the Revolution" for his ability to raise and manage money. Morris and John Hancock, the first person to sign the declaration, were members of the Maritime Committee. Jones felt that both men could help him advance in the ranks of naval officers. He had learned from experience that wealth and family connections were as important to achieving success in the colonies as they had been in England. Since he had neither, the next best thing would be to build strong support among committee members who were shaping the navy.

The *Providence* sailed from Philadelphia in late August. The sloop left the Chesapeake Bay and set a course toward Bermuda, which was in the main shipping lanes for vessels traveling to and from England.

Within a week, the *Providence* had captured an English merchant ship for a prize and sent it back to Philadelphia with a prize crew. A week later, in the waters near Bermuda, the *Providence* took two more cargo ships loaded with rum, sugar, ginger, and oil intended for wealthy Londoners. By the end of September, the *Providence* was low on crewmen because they had been put aboard the captured ships to sail the prizes back to land.

Jones decided to sail north toward Nova Scotia to attack any British ships there, and to recruit crew members in ports along the way. He met with success again in the frigid northern waters of the Atlantic Ocean. He captured several more prizes and burned several British ships that were anchored in the harbor at Halifax, Nova Scotia. In mid-October, after a cruise of just under two months, the *Providence* sailed into Narragansett Bay followed by four prize vessels. In all, Jones and his men had captured seven cargo ships.

What should have been a time of triumph for Jones and his men became instead a time of frustration. Half of the prize money went immediately to the navy. The other half was divided among the crew. Jones and the officers received a higher percentage than the seamen. Some of the crew who had sailed the prizes to port with captured crew and the cargo felt entitled to a bigger share than the crew who had remained aboard the *Providence*. For their part, the crew on the *Providence* had been at sea longer than those men who had sailed the prizes back to port and thus felt their share was well-deserved. In the end, the division of the money satisfied no one.

Some crewmen were so unhappy with their take that they deserted the navy to join privateers, where the pay was between $12 and $16 per month—twice the navy's pay—and a greater share of prize money. Adding to the loss of men was the American navy's policy of 12-month enlistment. Many experienced sailors left the navy after a year to serve aboard privateers where conditions and pay were better.

While he awaited orders for his next mission, Jones wrote a letter to Robert Morris in which he expressed his frustration with naval policy. In the letter, he warned Morris that unless some adjustments were made in prize money, the navy would never become a powerful military force. He added, "and without a respectable Navy...alas America."

Although Jones was personally dissatisfied with navy policies, he received praise from Hopkins for his successful cruise. Hopkins was one of the few men who was pleased with the division of prize money, because, although he remained in port, he received 5 percent of all prize money. The commodore recognized Jones's promise as a leader, and promoted him to command of the *Alfred*, the first naval ship on which Jones had served. Saltonstall, the ship's original captain, was promoted to commander of a new warship that had recently been completed in Philadelphia.

A little over a month after he sailed into Narragansett Bay with a fleet of four prizes, Jones sailed out in command of the *Alfred*. Before leaving, Jones had paid prize money out of his own pocket for additional food supplies such as molasses, sugar, peas, oatmeal, and pickled pig's heads, because he considered the navy's food rations inadequate. It was the first of several times during the war that Jones used his own money to improve conditions or pay his crew.

★

In December 1776, Thomas Paine wrote *The Crisis*, a pamphlet that attempted to raise the colonists' spirits.

★

The *Alfred* was under orders to sail north toward Nova Scotia and attack any British cargo ships bound for Canada. Within a week, the ship had taken one prize and sent it back to Rhode Island with a crew. Soon after that prize was taken, the *Alfred* captured an extremely valuable prize— the British cargo ship *Mellish*, which carried winter uniforms and other supplies intended for British troops. The large ship was sent directly to Rhode Island, and the uniforms were shipped to Washington's troops in time for use at the Battle of Trenton in December 1776.

After he captured two more prize ships, Jones headed for port with another successful mission completed. He and his crew had earned not only the respect of Hopkins, but a large payment of prize money to be divided.

In slightly less than a year as a naval officer, Jones had achieved a great deal of success. Though the men that served under him considered him a brutally strict commander, they had earned as much prize money as any crews in the navy at that time. Instead of being rewarded for his achievement, however, Jones suffered a bitter disappointment.

Far Down the List

During the time that Jones had been at sea, more than a dozen new warships were being built in shipyards from Baltimore, Maryland, to Portsmouth, New Hampshire. In addition, shipyards had repaired and converted a number of captured prize ships into warships. By early 1777, the American navy had 24 ships ready for command. Of those, 13 were new.

Jones was in Boston in January when he received word that Congress had drawn up a list of captains to command ships. He was ranked behind 17 other officers for a ship, which resulted in his reassignment to the *Providence*. Jones was outraged and insulted. He wrote to Robert Morris and other members of the Marine Committee to express his dismay.

P·REVERE

3 Martin.——4 Glasgow.——5 Mermaid.—6 Romney.—7 Lancefton.—8 Bonetta.

Boston Harbor was one of the busiest and most important ports in the colonies.

Once again, Jones learned, his lack of connections in the colonies had worked against him. Captains ahead of him on the list had been given command of ships that were built in cities where the captains had been born and raised. Crews for the ships had to be recruited from the region in which they were built, so having a ship under the command of a familiar officer helped in recruiting. It would have been extremely difficult for an outsider like Jones, especially with his reputation as a harsh leader, to raise a crew of as many as 250 men in an area where he was unknown.

59

Chapter 4

ACROSS THE
ATLANTIC

From the time he guided the *John* back to port as
a 21-year-old mate, Jones had taken great pride in
his knowledge of sailing and ability to command.
Nine years later, after two successful missions for
the American navy, he had been passed over for
command by men he considered inferior.

OPPOSITE: The battle between the *Drake* and the *Ranger*, under Jones, was
the first time an American ship went into battle flying the American flag.

61

Furious, Jones left Boston in the winter of 1777 and traveled to Philadelphia to speak directly to the Marine Committee. Although he was a man of strong opinions whose personality angered many people, Jones had two allies on the committee—Robert Morris and John Hancock. Both men felt that the navy could not afford to risk the resignation of an officer as skilled as Jones. Hancock wrote a note to Morris about his concerns over the treatment of Jones, stating, "I admire the spirited conduct of little Jones . . . and I am certain you wish him to be constantly active."

Jones made his case before the committee, and in the spring of 1777, the committee members gave him an opportunity. At that time, one of the largest shipbuilding cities in the United States was Portsmouth, New Hampshire. Builders there were about to complete construction of a three-mast warship called the *Ranger*. The captain who had originally been given command of the *Ranger* was caught selling goods that he had taken from a prize ship. The committee voted to replace the original commander of the *Ranger* with Jones.

The committee's plan was to send Jones and the *Ranger* to France to deliver instructions from the Continental Congress to Benjamin Franklin, the American minister in Paris. At that time, in early 1777, France was secretly aiding the United States with money and some arms. Franklin and several other well-known Americans, including John Adams, were in Paris to obtain more money and

Portsmouth, New Hampshire, was an important center of shipbuilding during the Revolution.

attempt to persuade France to join the war against England. They could not negotiate aid packages or sign agreements, though, without specific orders from Congress.

The committee instructed Jones to remain in European waters once he had delivered the congressional instructions. Using French ports as a base, Jones was to harass British merchant ships in the English Channel and the North Sea, off the English coast.

Off to Europe

Jones spent most of the spring and summer of 1777 in Portsmouth, preparing the *Ranger* for its initial voyage. The ship was slightly smaller than the *Alfred*—about 110 feet long—with 20 nine-pound

63

cannons and a crew of 150, including marines. It was difficult to find enough men to sail the ship, since many experienced seamen had signed on with privateers, and Jones's departure was delayed until well into the fall.

Finally, on November 1, 1777, the *Ranger* left Portsmouth for France. The delayed departure was fortunate for the Americans in one way: Jones was able to bring word to Franklin and the others about the important American victory at Saratoga, New York, on October 7. American leaders hoped that news of that victory would finally convince the French government and King Louis XVI to join the war.

In early December, the *Ranger* arrived in the port city of Nantes, France. The *Ranger*'s first voyage had shown Jones that the ship's masts and rigging needed adjustment. He made arrangements for his crew to work on the ship while he traveled overland to Paris. Before he left port, Jones ordered large supplies of fresh food, which he paid for from his own pocket, for his men.

In Paris, Jones went directly to meet Franklin. The Philadelphia publisher, inventor, and scientist was the most famous American of his time. *Poor Richard's Almanac*, his collections of witty advice and sayings, was a best-seller in France and throughout Europe.

The two men, Jones slightly over 30, and Franklin, more than 70 years old, became friends immediately. Franklin supported and praised Jones

Poor Richard, 1740.

AN

Almanack

For the Year of Chrift

1740,

Being LEAP YEAR.

And makes fince the Creation — Years.

By the Account of the Eaftern *Greeks* — 7248
By the Latin Church, when ⊙ ent. ♈ — 6939
By the Computation of *W. W.* — 5749
By the *Roman* Chronology — 5689
By the *Jewifh* Rabbies — 5501

Wherein is contained,

The Lunations, Eclipfes, Judgment of the Weather, Spring Tides, Planets Motions & mutual Afpects, Sun and Moon's Rifing and Setting, Length of Days, Time of High Water, Fairs, Courts, and obfervable Days.

Fitted to the Latitude of Forty Degrees, and a Meridian of Five Hours Weft from *London*, but may without fenfible Error, ferve all the adjacent Places, even from *Newfoundland* to *South-Carolina*.

By RICHARD SAUNDERS, Philom.

PHILADELPHIA:

Printed and fold by *B. FRANKLIN*, at the New Printing-Office near the Market.

Poor Richard's Almanack was second only to the Bible in sales throughout the American colonies.

in letters back to Congress for the rest of the captain's career. Jones, for his part, considered Franklin the wisest man he had ever met.

The news of the American victory at Saratoga set events in motion in Paris. In early 1778, France signed an alliance agreement with the new United States. The French agreed to provide money, supplies, troops, and warships to aid the fight against their bitter enemies, the English.

Raids on English Ports

By that time, Jones had returned to Nantes and his repaired ship. While in Paris, he and Franklin decided that instead of taking merchant prizes, the *Ranger* should raid English ports to destroy shipping and, if possible, take English hostages. Such raids, Franklin believed, would force the British navy to keep some of its warships in English waters rather than sending them to fight in American territory. The hostages would be exchanged for captured American sailors.

Jones's orders did not go over well with his crew. They had been recruited with the promise of money from captured prizes. Destroying English shipping would not bring in extra money, they complained. Jones replied that he had received permission from Franklin to offer the men a bonus for the mission, and even paid some of the money from his pocket once again. Crew members reluctantly agreed to make the journey, but relations between the Scottish captain and his American crew were strained. Several men deserted the ship to find work as privateers.

In early April 1778, the *Ranger* set sail from Nantes. The gun ports of the ship were draped with canvas to disguise it as a merchant ship. Jones set a course for the English port he knew best—Whitehaven. There he planned to burn as many ships as possible and lead a landing party to capture hostages.

The daring raid did not begin well. The wind died down as the *Ranger* closed in on Whitehaven, which stopped the ship miles from the harbor at about midnight on April 20.

Privateers earned a larger share of prize money from captured ships, which caused many American sailors to desert.

Jones had no option but to launch two landing boat crews—about 40 men— and row all night to the docks. The exhausted Americans arrived at about 5 o'clock and immediately disabled the cannons that overlooked the harbor. One member of the crew was a traitor who had signed on at Portsmouth in order to get home to England. As the Americans spiked the cannons—drove metal spikes into the fuse holes—

67

the turncoat ran through the streets of Whitehaven knocking on doors and shouting out warnings.

Soon, hundreds of townspeople rushed to the docks, where Jones had set one ship on fire. He realized that he and his men had to escape. The Americans scrambled onto their boats and rowed away. The British attempted to fire on them, but their cannons were useless.

In the spring of 1778, France negotiated a treaty with the United States that recognized the former colonies as an independent country.

The raid on Whitehaven did little damage to property, but it shocked the British. No foreigners had attacked English soil in more than a century. Word of the incident spread rapidly.

The crew of the *Ranger* knew nothing of the effect of their small attack. Jones was disappointed that he had not had time to destroy more ships or take any hostages.

He decided to stage an attack on St. Mary's Isle, a small peninsula in the Solway Firth, not far from the Craik estate, where he had spent his childhood. St. Mary's Isle was owned by the earl of Selkirk, a wealthy aristocrat who had built a large stone mansion that overlooked the firth. Jones believed that taking such a wealthy man hostage might lead to the release of a good number of American prisoners.

St. Mary's Isle was less than a day's sailing distance from Whitehaven. Jones arrived early the next day and dropped anchor offshore. He led a landing boat to the shore below the mansion. The occupants of the Selkirk residence were just waking up when they saw the group entering the grounds. Jones's men cornered a servant and demanded to be taken to the earl. The earl, however, had left the day before for London.

With no hostage to take, Jones ordered his men to return to the boat before word spread of their location. The landing party replied that they wanted to ransack the mansion. Since they could not capture seagoing prizes, they demanded the right to steal any valuables. Jones did not want to risk a mutiny, so he gave permission as long as no one was harmed.

As the sun rose, the earl's wife, Lady Selkirk, their children, and numerous household staff watched helplessly as what she called "horrid-looking wretches" stole her finest silver and dashed away. No sooner had they left than a mob of local citizens, alerted to the invasion, arrived. Twice within 48 hours, Jones and his men had dared to set foot in England.

Though little harm had been done in either raid, Jones was soon a topic of conversation as news— and so-called eyewitness stories—of his daring attacks spread across the countryside. Newspapers published articles about the attack of "privateers" on "defenceless" English ports. Perhaps the greatest shock came when someone in Whitehaven recognized John Paul, once a local apprentice, as the leader of the raid. The traitor from the *Ranger*'s crew then identified him by name as John Paul Jones.

First Naval Battle

The *Ranger* was soon under full sail along the eastern coast of Ireland, with plans to sail around to the west coast before turning south for France. Word about the American ship in English waters had spread rapidly, and British ships in the region were on the lookout for a three-mast sloop. In late April, several days after Jones's landings, the British warship *Drake* caught sight of a vessel that matched the description of the *Ranger*.

Jones had spotted the *Drake,* in turn, and recognized it as a British man-of-war about the size of the *Ranger*. As the *Drake* approached, Jones ordered most of his crew to hide below the decks. He turned his stern to the oncoming ship, so the enemy could not see the *Ranger*'s gun ports. He then slowed the ship, and allowed the *Drake* to close in. As it came within shouting range, a voice called from the *Drake*, "What ship is that?"

Suddenly, Jones ordered the American flag raised. "The American ship *Ranger*," he called back. Then he added a challenge: "We are waiting for you."

Jones quickly turned the *Ranger* so that its broadside faced the bow of the *Drake*. His gunners fired a broadside of chainshot and grapeshot along the deck of the *Drake*, which ripped its sails and tore huge splinters from the masts. The battle was on.

Although Jones had commanded the capture of many cargo ships, the battle with the *Drake* was his first battle with an enemy warship. It was also the first time an American ship went into battle under the Stars and Stripes flag of the United States.

Jones's sailing skills enabled him to immediately maneuver his ship to gain advantage over the *Drake*. After the *Ranger*'s first broadside, Jones turned his ship so that the wind struck its sails with enough force to tilt it back at a slight angle, facing the enemy. This meant that his cannons were aimed at the deck and rigging of the *Drake*. Firing grapeshot and chainshot, he disabled the British warship without damaging its hull and sinking the ship. The *Drake*, on the other hand, could only fire light six-pound cannonballs that bounced off the *Ranger*'s hull.

Jones fights an enemy sailor in a fanciful drawing that appeared in a book about his life.

Within an hour, the captain and first officer of the *Drake* were dead. The crew struck colors—lowered their flag in surrender. The *Ranger* had lost two men but had suffered little damage. The Americans took more than 130 British prisoners, and towed the *Drake*, the only prize of the journey, to France.

71

Chapter 5

THE WAIT AND
THE GREAT BATTLE

B y the time the *Ranger* entered the French
harbor of Brest in May 1778, Jones had proven
himself one of the most skilled commanders of the
American navy. Jones now had great plans to lead
a squadron of ships and a huge force of French
troops in an invasion of England. Instead, he
remained ashore and inactive for nearly nine
months. The obstacles he faced in returning to sea
were a clear example of the problems faced by the
entire American navy during the war.

Opposite: The battle between the *Bonhomme Richard* and the *Serapis*
was the greatest naval battle of the Revolution.

73

Jones's first task was to pay his men for their service. To do this, he once again used his own money, because the American government was having difficulty raising funds to even pay its troops in the United States. Jones knew it might be months before pay arrived from the U.S. treasury. He wanted to stay on good terms with his men, so he paid them from his own funds, and believed the government would later pay him back.

Next, Jones wanted to sell the *Drake* to the French government and split the prize money among his men. That took several months, and in the end, Jones received much less from the French than he thought the British warship was worth. There were many complaints among the officers and crew of the *Ranger* about the prize money. Jones asked Franklin to write to Congress and ask for a bonus for each man who had been in the landing parties at Whitehaven and St. Mary's Isle. Franklin and the other American ministers rejected the request—again because of a shortage of funds.

The money disputes kept the Americans ashore until late in the summer of 1778. By that time, most of the crew was near the end of the 12-month enlistment term. As much as he tried to keep his crew satisfied, Jones remained unpopular because of his strict discipline and the fact that he was still perceived as a foreigner.

Rather than have the crew abandon the *Ranger* in France, the American ministers ordered the ship to return to America. Naval losses in U.S. waters in

1778 had given the British complete control of the American coast. The British were able to move troops and supplies along the coast without interference. A warship of the *Ranger*'s size was desperately needed in home waters.

By the time the *Ranger* arrived back in Portsmouth, the ministers knew, a year's enlistment would be up, but a new crew could be recruited. Jones, who hoped for command of a larger ship or even a squadron, remained in France while the *Ranger* sailed home.

It proved difficult, however, to gain command of a fighting ship. In September, Franklin made arrangements for Jones to take command of a converted merchant ship named *L'Indien* that was docked in France. Before Jones could reach the ship, the French sold it to a commander from South Carolina who had come to Europe to obtain ships for his state's private naval force.

Benjamin Franklin was minister to France during the Revolution.

For several months, Jones wrote letters to French nobles and other influential men—including King Louis XVI—requesting a ship. He even offered to arrange a personal loan and pay for a ship with his borrowed money.

Franklin and the other American ministers in France were sympathetic to Jones, but they faced serious problems of their own. As they tried to get loans from European governments to pay for the war at home, they had to compete with representatives from South Carolina, Virginia, and other states that sought their own funds and military support.

Over several months, the French offered Jones some British prizes that had been brought to the country. Those ships were in need of repair and did not appeal to Jones. In his letter refusing the broken-down vessels, Jones wrote, "I wish no connection with any ship that does not sail fast, for I intend to go in harm's way." Jones's expression "in harm's way" has been used in military writing ever since he coined it.

A Ship for Jones

Finally, in early 1779, Jones received word that the French government had a large merchant ship it would be willing to outfit with several dozen cannons for him. This vessel was named *Le Duc de Duras*, but Jones changed the name of the ship once he took command. To honor the American he most admired, Jones named the ship after

Jones named his new ship *Bonhomme Richard* to honor Benjamin Franklin's book *Poor Richards's Almanack*.

Franklin's famous work. ("Poor Richard" was "Bonhomme Richard" in French.)

At more than 250 feet in length and carrying 40 cannons, the *Bonhomme Richard* was much larger than any vessel Jones had ever commanded. It took nearly six months to outfit the ship with its guns, replace rotted planks, convert it to a warship with battle stations in the top rigging, and recruit the 380 crewmen and marines that were needed for the cruise.

As he worked on the *Bonhomme Richard*, Jones received word that the American ministers and the French wanted him to command a squadron of ships and sail into English waters. The ships under Jones would take on British warships in addition to attacking merchant vessels. The plan was for Jones to cause enough trouble to force the British to recall some warships from the American coast to protect England.

In addition to the *Bonhomme Richard*, the American ship the *Alliance*, which had arrived in France in 1779, and three French ships were placed under Jones's command. The French government paid for the outfitting of all the ships, except for the *Alliance*. Thus, while Jones sailed under the American flag, the French paid his expenses.

The crew of the *Bonhomme Richard* was recruited from several sources. American officers and some crewmen were freed from British prisons in exchange for the prisoners Jones had taken on the *Drake*. A large number of crew were Irish or

English sailors who hated King George and supported the American cause. Some were Portuguese fishermen who also supported the Americans. The marines on board were well-trained French troops. Many crewmen signed on because they wanted to sail under Jones, whose fame, at least in Europe, had spread widely.

The *Bonhomme Richard*, leading a squadron of five ships, set sail in August 1779. Jones's ship, the largest, carried 40 cannons: 6 eighteen-pounders, 28 twelve-pounders, and 6 nine-pounders. The ship's crew of 380, including 137 French marines, was drawn from seven countries, but most of the men were American or British.

A conflict immediately arose between Jones and the captain of the American ship *Alliance*, Pierre Landais. Landais was 10 years older than Jones and a lifelong sailor. He had left the French navy and gone to America at the outbreak of the war to seek a commission in the new American navy.

Landais was not only given command of an American ship, he became friends with Samuel Adams, who made Landais an

Samuel Adams (pictured) became friends with Jones's rival, Pierre Landais.

John Paul Jones

honorary citizen of Massachusetts. Thus, Landais was the only American commander in the squadron. Landais let it be known from the beginning of the mission that he would not obey orders from a so-called foreigner such as Jones. The two men quickly became enemies.

Over the first month of the mission, Jones's squadron sailed north along the west coast of Ireland and around the northern point of Scotland. The fleet took several British prizes, and by the middle of September was sailing south along the eastern coast of England. By that time, two of the smaller French ships had returned to France because they needed repairs and their crews had left to serve as prize crews. The *Alliance*, under Landais, making its own way and capturing prizes, sailed far ahead of the other two ships, *Bonhomme Richard* and *Pallas*.

By this time, the British navy had word that Jones was sailing in English waters, although they did not know exactly where. Several British warships combed the region off the west coast of the country, near Whitehaven—the opposite side of England from Jones's location. On land, the alarm spread from Scotland south that the coast was in danger of another attack by Jones. Coastal defenses were on full alert in every area of the country.

On September 22, the *Bonhomme Richard* was in coastal waters off Flamborough Head, a peninsula on the west coast of England. Jones had sighted a merchant convoy, counted more than 41 sails on the horizon, and was in pursuit of any stragglers. A captured local sailor informed Jones that two warships escorted the convoy. One, the *Countess of Scarborough*, carried 20 guns. The other, much larger ship, the *Serapis*, was believed to carry 44 guns.

The *Serapis*, commanded by Captain Richard Pearson, was a new copper-bottomed man-of-war. The copper made the huge ship slip speedily through the water, an advantage over slower wooden-bottomed boats such as Jones's. The *Serapis* carried 50 guns, including 20 eighteen-pounders on a gun deck below the main deck—more than three times as many 18-pounders as Jones's ship.

The Legendary Battle

During this mission—and on others—Jones had frequently sailed with the British flag flying from his stern. Because ships were often captured or traded hands, there was no way to tell from which country a vessel actually came. The *Bonhomme Richard* had sailed through British waters flying the British Union Jack. Because of this deception, Pearson had to sail his ship close enough to call out to Jones. Even then, Jones gave a false name for his ship to confuse Pearson and draw the *Serapis* closer for a broadside.

By 6:30 on the evening of September 23, 1779, the two ships were within a pistol shot of each other. The other ships—*Pallas*, *Alliance*, and the

Countess of Scarborough—were in the vicinity, but not close enough to do battle. The sun was setting, and the waters were calm as the French marines scrambled to their battle stations at the top of the masts. Gun crews were at their stations, with guns primed and matches lit.

Moments after Pearson's final warning, the American flag was hoisted about the decks of the *Bonhomme Richard*, and the battle began. Both ships fired broadsides at each other. The crews reloaded, but at the second broadside, two of Jones's 18-pounders exploded, killing many crewmen and destroying part of the top deck.

★

The Continental army spent much of 1779 in camp because of a severe shortage of shoes.

★

Jones quickly saw that his ship would not win a battle of broadsides because the *Serapis* had too much firepower. He used all of his sailing knowledge to try to maneuver the *Bonhomme Richard* across the bow or the stern of the *Serapis* to avoid the enemy broadside. Pearson, however, was just as clever and matched Jones move for move. Meanwhile, the cannons roared.

At that moment, early in the battle, the *Bonhomme Richard* was suddenly hit by a broadside to its stern, which sent splinters flying through the air and tore the American flag from its post. Jones thought that the *Countess of Scarborough* had joined the battle and swung his telescope to see the enemy ship's location. Instead of a British ship, he saw the *Alliance*. Landais, who was by that time believed to be insane, had fired on Jones.

82

Within minutes of the first broadside, the *Bonhomme Richard* was in serious danger of being blasted from the water. Jones knew that his ship's guns could not compete with those of the *Serapis*. His only alternative was to bring his ship hull to hull with Pearson's ship to stifle the cannons.

In Jones's first attempt to come close to the *Serapis*, his ship's bow rammed the stern of the British ship. With a close view of the damaged American ship, Pearson believed that he had the advantage. He saw that the *Bonhomme Richard*'s American flag was gone, and he called out to Jones. "Have you struck your colors?"

The question of whether he had surrendered enraged Jones. He shouted back one of the most famous phrases of the war: "I have not yet begun to fight!"

True to his word, Jones immediately maneuvered his ship away from the *Serapis* and tried another approach. This one worked—the *Serapis* could not back away from the collision, and soon the sides of the ships were touching in bow to stern position.

"Well done, my brave lads," Jones shouted to his crew. "Throw on board her the grappling irons and stand by for boarding."

For the next two hours, as a full moon rose over the calm ocean waters, one of the fiercest naval battles ever fought took place. From their battle stations high in the masts, French marines fired muskets and threw grenades onto the deck of the *Serapis*. Dead British sailors were scattered across

83

The two ships were so close that the *Serapis* could not open its gunports.

the deck. The British ship was so close that its outward opening gunports could not be raised. The gunners, ordered to fire anyway, blasted open their ship's ports and sent canister shot whistling across the deck of the *Bonhomme Richard*.

The battle caused the sails of both ships to burst into flames, and the fighting stopped briefly while the fires were put out. Later, the fighting resumed, and Pearson ordered his 18-pounders, protected in a gun area below the main deck, to fire at will.

Soon the decks of the *Bonhomme Richard* were splintered and slippery with blood. On the decks of the *Serapis* more than a dozen fires, sparked by grenades, burned. By this point, the *Bonhomme Richard* leaned so closely against the *Serapis* that the crosspieces on its masts—called yards—hung over the decks of the British ship. French marines jumped from their positions in the rigging of the

John Paul Jones

Bonhomme Richard to the mast tops of the *Serapis* and fired straight down at sailors on the deck of the British ship.

While this struggle was taking place, the *Pallas* and the *Countess of Scarborough* exchanged broadsides several miles away. At the same time, Landais and his ship circled the main battle. Rather than helping Jones, however, Landais ordered two more broadsides fired into

Dozens of fires burned on the decks of the connected ships.

the *Bonhomme Richard*. The cannonballs killed many of Jones's crew and blasted several holes in the ship below the waterline. Soon the *Bonhomme Richard* was sinking—due to fire from an ally ship.

As the battle entered its third hour, Jones took over as gunner on a nine-pound cannon that had been moved on deck. Nearly half his crew was dead or wounded, and there was five feet of water in the shattered hull of his ship. Suddenly, amidst the gunfire and flames, Jones heard one of his

What Did Jones Really Say?

Though he was successful and widely respected during his naval career, John Paul Jones is mainly remembered today for the words "I have not yet begun to fight!"

It is not certain, however, that those were Jones's actual words. In his own account of the battle, he did not give the exact phrase he used. When asked if he had surrendered, Jones wrote, "I . . . answered him in the most determined negative . . . [and] renewed the battle with double fury."

Soon after the battle, several British crew members of the *Bonhomme Richard* deserted the ship in a small boat. They rowed to shore and were soon telling the story of the famous battle in great detail. A newspaper account of the story told by these men gives a different reply. When asked if he had struck his colors, Jones's reply was reported as, "No. I have not yet thought of it, but am determined to make you strike."

Jones's famous phrase first appeared in a biography of him written in 1825. The author interviewed Richard Dale, a man who had served as a lieutenant under Jones during the battle. Dale, more than 45 years after the battle, recalled that Jones's reply to Pearson was, "I have not yet begun to fight!"

officers order a crewman to strike the colors. Jones flew into a rage and threw a pistol at the officer, which hit him in the head and knocked him out. "I will sink, but I will never strike," Jones shouted.

Moments later, luck found Jones once again. One of his men in the top yards threw down a grenade that bounced off the deck and into the powder magazine of the *Serapis*. There was a huge explosion belowdecks at the same moment that Jones fired his nine-pounder. The chainshot from that gun cut the main mast of the *Serapis* in half. Within minutes, the *Serapis* was in as serious a situation as the *Bonhomme Richard*. Pearson, however, did not have Jones's iron will. He struck his colors, and surrendered to the Americans after four hours of fighting. Both captains had lost more that half their crewmen in the bloodiest naval battle of the Revolution.

As the sun rose on September 24, Jones ordered his crew to abandon ship and board the *Serapis*. On board, they worked with the British prisoners to rig a temporary mainmast. As the *Bonhomme Richard* sank, Jones guided the badly damaged *Serapis* to the closet friendly port, Texel, an island off the coast of Holland. He was followed by the *Pallas*, which had captured the *Countess of Scarborough*. The *Alliance* had already sailed far ahead.

Chapter 6

A FORGOTTEN HERO

As news of the battle between the *Bonhomme Richard* and the *Serapis* spread, Jones became one of the most honored—and feared—men in Europe. In England, while British naval commanders said he was nothing more than a pirate, common people composed songs to honor his bravery. Despite the fact that he was an enemy, his Scottish peasant background made him seem more British that American. Books about his adventures—with titles such as *The True History of John Paul Jones, the Notorious Sea Pirate*—soon appeared, and many fanciful tales about his life arose from them.

OPPOSITE: French troops landed in Rhode Island in 1780 to aid the Continental army.

In Holland, where he had landed, crowds followed Jones down the street and sang songs about his bravery. In France, Jones was the most honored man in Paris, and received a medal of bravery and a specially made sword from King Louis XVI. Painters and sculptors begged him to pose for them.

For Jones, however, the glory was secondary to his two main concerns: paying his crew and dealing with the treachery of Landais. After word of the captain's actions aboard the *Alliance* reached Benjamin Franklin, John Adams, and Arthur Lee, the American ministers to France, Landais was relieved of command. Jones was given command of the *Alliance*, and he formed a crew for it that consisted of the survivors of the *Bonhomme Richard* and members of Landais's original crew.

As the winter of 1779–1780 began, the British navy set up a blockade along the French and Dutch coasts. The goal was to prevent those countries from sending military supplies to the United States—and to keep Jones from making further voyages into English waters.

Meanwhile, in the United States, the war was not going well for the Americans. British troops aboard ships could move up and down the American coast without opposition. The British general Henry Clinton had left the British stronghold in New York City, sailed south, and taken Charleston Harbor in a battle that destroyed the few remaining ships in the American navy. The

British military plan was give up the New England states and to conquer the southern states, which were the wealthiest. By 1780, the plan seemed to be working, and Americans were desperate for any hopeful news. Thus, when accounts of the battle off Flamborough Head eventually reached America, the news became one of the few bright spots in a dismal year.

Word of the Americans' serious situation had reached Paris. French troops under General Jean-Baptiste-Donatien de Vimeur, Count de Rochambeau had beaten the blockade and sailed to Rhode Island. Still, the Americans remained terribly short of guns, gunpowder, and most other military supplies. Franklin and Adams felt that the best way to help was to send Jones back to America in command of the *Alliance*. That ship, along with several cargo ships, was ordered to carry supplies to Washington.

The mission was scheduled to depart with the first favorable winds in the spring of 1780. In mid-April, the *Alliance* was able to evade the blockade and sail to Lorient, a port in southern France to await supplies and other ships. It was then that the plans fell apart.

By that time, the crew on the *Alliance*—both the original members and those from the *Bonhomme Richard*—had not been paid in nearly a year. Now, Jones was asking them to embark on a dangerous ocean crossing. It was too

★

In May 1780, American soldiers surrendered the city of Charleston to British generals Clinton and Cornwallis.

★

91

much—the men refused to sail unless they were paid their salary plus their share of the prize money. Jones was forced to leave the *Alliance* and make a long overland voyage back to Paris. There he pleaded for funds and awaited the sale of the prizes taken in the cruise of 1779.

While Jones was away, Landais surfaced again. He arrived in Lorient with the one American minister who disliked both Jones and Franklin— Arthur Lee. Landais convinced the men on the *Alliance* that, because of his American connections, he would be able to obtain a salary for them in Philadelphia. Most of the original *Alliance* crew accepted Landais at his word. The others, from the *Bonhomme Richard*, did not. Those men were abruptly put ashore. On June 20, hours before Jones returned from Paris, Landais and the *Alliance* left port. Although the ship's cargo included some military supplies, it consisted mainly of the personal possessions of Arthur Lee, who planned to return to Philadelphia. There he intended to discredit Franklin and Jones by accusing them of misspending American prize money.

A Lost Year

With the *Alliance* gone, there was little Jones could do but complain about the actions of Landais and Lee. Franklin was furious with Lee, but he was also anxious to get the supplies that Landais had left behind to America as quickly as possible. By that time, a warship named the *Ariel* had docked at

Lorient, and Franklin arranged to have Jones take command of the ship and carry the important cargo to Washington.

There was so much cargo that the *Ariel* had to be completely overhauled from a warship to a cargo ship. This process lasted through the summer and into the fall of 1780. The *Ariel* finally left Lorient in late September. Jones's bad luck continued when the ship ran into a powerful storm just off the coast of France. The wind was so strong that it snapped the masts of the *Ariel*, and only Jones's great skills as a sailor enabled the ship to return to port.

Repairs took several months, and it was late 1780 before Jones set out again. In February 1781,

Philadelphia was a center of activity during the Revolution.

the *Ariel* sailed into Philadelphia with several hundred tons of badly needed guns, ammunition, and uniforms for Washington's army. In port, Jones learned that the crew of the *Alliance* had revolted against Landais the previous summer because of his increasingly irrational actions. The captain had been court-martialed and dishonorably discharged from the navy. Lee had been shamed by his decision to bring his personal belongings home rather than weapons. He returned to his home in disgrace.

Triumph and Disappointment

By the time Jones arrived in Philadelphia, he was a war hero. Congress voted a resolution of thanks to him for his service, but Jones was more interested in being paid than in being thanked. He had not been paid by the U.S. government since 1775, the year he had entered the service. He had paid for his lodgings and for his crew from his own funds and through loans from wealthy French nobility.

By Jones's calculations, the U.S. government owed him more than $20,000—a huge sum at that time. That figure did not even take into account the prize money from the cruises on the *Ranger* and the *Bonhomme Richard* that had not been settled. Jones spent much of the spring and summer of 1781 in Philadelphia speaking to Robert Morris, John Hancock, and other lawmakers about arranging some payment.

Jones was also interested in taking command of another ship and returning to action. By 1781,

94

Cornwallis surrendered to Washington on October 19, 1781.

however, all American warships had been captured, destroyed, or were trapped in port. The only ship available was being built in Portsmouth. This was the ship *America*, a 200-foot, 74-gun warship that its builder hoped would become the greatest warship on the seas. In August, Congress voted to award command of the *America* to Jones, and he left for the long journey north to New Hampshire. He had been in Portsmouth several days when word arrived of the American and French victory over General Lord Charles Cornwallis at Yorktown, Virginia. With this defeat, more than

95

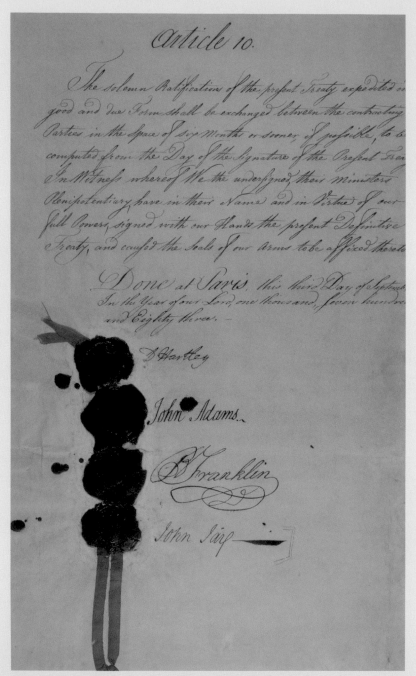

The Treaty of Paris, which officially ended the Revolution, was signed in 1783.

one-third of the British army in America was disarmed. It was the final major battle of the Revolution.

Jones was gratified to learn that many of the American troops had fought with weapons brought over by the *Ariel*. He also believed that the war might continue at sea. For that reason, he was eager to get the *America* completed and set sail. Once again, however, Jones faced disappointment, this time the bitterest of his career.

At the end of the Revolution, Congress faced a huge number of bills, but because there was no strong central government with the power to tax citizens, there was no way to raise money. In 1782, the new nation's financial situation became so serious that Congress voted to sell *America* to France to raise cash. Jones was ready to take the ship on its maiden voyage when he learned that a French commander would soon arrive to take command.

In late 1782, Jones received the back pay and expenses owed to him by the U.S. government. Ironically, some of the money was raised from the sale of the *America*. Jones's naval career for the United States was over by the time the Treaty of Paris officially ended the war in 1783.

Jones was a popular figure
during the Revolution, but he
was quickly forgotten afterward.

Epilogue

Jones spent much of his time in the years immediately after the war in France. He worked with Thomas Jefferson, the new American minister to France, in an attempt to settle the issue of the prize money for himself and his crews. At the same time, he continued to write to American lawmakers with requests for a command from Congress. He had no success. No ships were being built, and few of the existing ships were seaworthy.

In 1785, the prize money from the sale of the ships and goods taken under Jones's command was finally awarded. Jones received some money, but his officers and crew received less than they were due. Some of the money was used to pay the salaries of Jefferson and other Americans in Paris, and part of it went into the American treasury.

In 1788, after repeated failures to get a command from the United States, Jones served in the Russian navy as a fleet commander in Russia's war with Turkey. After he led his ships to victory in a large battle on the Black Sea, Jones began to suffer health problems. He left Russia and returned to Paris. He lived there until 1792, when he died from kidney disease at the age of 45.

John Paul Jones was placed in an coffin filled with alcohol to preserve his body in as complete a state as possible. He was then buried in an unmarked grave in Paris, where his body remained for more than a century. Although imaginary tales of his adventures were described in books and

99

The tomb of John Paul Jones lies in the chapel of the United States Naval Academy in Annapolis, Maryland.

recalled in songs, he was for the most part a forgotten hero of the American Revolution until 1905, when President Theodore Roosevelt ordered a search for Jones's burial place. Like Jones, Roosevelt believed that a navy was critically important for the national defense of any country. He also felt that Jones had not been given the respect he was due for his contributions to the early navy.

When Jones's grave was located, Roosevelt sent an American cruiser to France to retrieve the coffin. Jones's body was then brought back to the U.S. Naval Academy in Annapolis, Maryland, where it now lies in a place of honor in the academy chapel. The poor Scotsman who left home as a cabin boy at age 13 is now known as the "Father of the United States Navy."

Glossary

apprentice one who agrees to work under an experienced person to learn a skill or trade

blockade isolate an enemy by means of troops or ships

cat-o'-nine tails whip with multiple ends used to administer punishment

commander military leader

commission appointment of an officer to a high rank in the armies and navies of the eighteenth century

mast long vertical pole above the deck of a sailing ship that supports rigging, yards, and sails

Parliament legislative division of English government, made up of the House of Commons and the House of Lords

plantation large farm where one primary crop is grown, usually worked by slaves

privateer armed ship permitted by one government to attack enemy merchant shipping

skirmishes minor or preliminary conflicts or disputes

yard cross piece on a mast for holding sails

For More Information

Books

Lutz, Norma Jean. *John Paul Jones: Father of the U.S. Navy.* New York: Chelsea House, 1999.

Syme, Ronald. *Captain John Paul Jones, America's Fighting Seaman.* New York: Morrow, 1968.

Tibbits, Alison Davis. *John Paul Jones: Father of the American Navy.* Springfield, NJ: Enslow, 2002.

Zadra, Dan. *John Paul Jones, Naval Hero.* Mankato, MN: Creative Press, 1988.

Web Sites

Extracts from the Journals of My Campaigns: John Paul Jones
http://www.americanrevolution.org/jpj.html
Dictated and compiled primary source material

John Paul Jones
http://www.seacoastnh.com/jpj/
A good set of links for naval history

John Paul Jones
http://web2.iadfw.net/lrs/jones.HTML
A short biography

John Paul Jones Birthplace Museum
http://www.jpj.demon.co.uk/index.htm
Good background information with links to other historical information

Index